D0248023

THE VERY BEST OF
PAUL COOKSON

Let No One Steal Your Dreams
and Other Poems

Paul Cookson has been a poet for over thirty years, has written and edited over sixty collections, sold over a million books and visited thousands of schools, libraries and festivals all over the world.

Poet in Residence for the National Football Museum, Everton in the Community and Poet Laureate for Slade, he is also resident writer for Sing Together and Chant Productions, as well as a National Poetry Day Ambassador.

For more information and for bookings see paulcooksonpoet.co.uk or follow him on Twitter @paulcooksonpoet

CANCELLED
527 074 39 4

Other books by Paul Cookson

Paul Cookson's Joke Shop
Very Funny Poems
By Paul Cookson

100 Brilliant Poems for Children
Chosen by Paul Cookson

The Works
Every Kind of Poem You Will
Ever Need at School
Chosen by Paul Cookson

The Works 3
A Poet for Every Week of the Year
Chosen by Paul Cookson

THE VERY BEST OF PAUL COOKSON

Let No One Steal Your Dreams and other poems

MACMILLAN CHILDREN'S BOOKS

This book is dedicated to my mum – who took over fifty years to mention that she once spoke to Judy Garland.

Special thanks to Sally, Gaby Morgan, Stan Cullimore, Henry Priestman, Les Glover, Gill Faurie, Sean Ruane, Mick Shepherd, Helen Turner, Michael McDermott, Heather Horton, Don Powell, Jim and Frank Lea, Richard Kenyon, Mo Maghazachi and Mick King.

First published 2018 by Macmillan Children's Books
an imprint of Pan Macmillan
20 New Wharf Road, London N1 9RR
Associated companies throughout the world
www.panmacmillan.com

ISBN 978-1-5098-8349-3

Copyright © Paul Cookson 2018

The poem 'Home' was commissioned by Everton Football Club for their 2018 season ticket campaign and the accompanying film can be seen on line.

The right of Paul Cookson to be identified as the author of this work has been asserted by him in accordance with the Copyright, Designs and Patents Act 1988.

All rights reserved. No part of this publication may be reproduced, stored in a retrieval system, or transmitted, in any form or by any means (electronic, mechanical, photocopying, recording or otherwise), without the prior written permission of the publisher.

Pan Macmillan does not have any control over, or any responsibility for, any author or third-party websites referred to in or on this book.

1 3 5 7 9 8 6 4 2

A CIP catalogue record for this book is available from the British Library.

Printed and bound by CPI Group (UK) Ltd, Croydon CR0 4YY

This book is sold subject to the condition that it shall not, by way of trade or otherwise, be lent, resold, hired out, or otherwise circulated without the publisher's prior consent in any form of binding or cover other than that in which it is published and without a similar condition including this condition being imposed on the subsequent purchaser.

Contents

Let No One Steal Your Dreams

Let no one steal your dreams
Let no one tear apart
The burning of ambition
That fires the drive inside your heart

Let no one steal your dreams
Let no one tell you that you can't
Let no one hold you back
Let no one tell you that you won't

Set your sights and keep them fixed
Set your sights on high
Let no one steal your dreams
Your only limit is the sky

Let no one steal your dreams
Follow your heart
Follow your soul
For only when you follow them
Will you feel truly whole

Set your sights and keep them fixed
Set your sights on high
Let no one steal your dreams
Your only limit is the sky

May You Always

May your smile be ever present
May your skies be always blue
May your path be ever upward
May your heart be ever true

May your dreams be full to bursting
May your steps be always sure
May the fire in your soul
Blaze on for evermore

May you live to meet ambition
May you strive to pass each test
May you find the love your life deserves
May you always have the best

May your happiness be plentiful
May your regrets be few
May you always be my best friend
May you always . . . just be you

A Favourite Book and a Comfy Chair

I just can't wait to be with you
Time flies by when you are there
You take me to another place
A favourite book and a comfy chair

You fill my head with images
And feelings I can't wait to share
You touch all my emotions
A favourite book and a comfy chair

Where you go I follow
You can take me anywhere
Horizons disappear with you . . .
A favourite book and a comfy chair

Invisible Magicians

Thanks be to all magicians
The ones we never see
Who toil away both night and day
Weaving spells for you and me

The ones who paint the rainbows
The ones who salt the seas
The ones who purify the dew
And freshen up the breeze

The ones who brighten lightning
The ones who whiten snow
The ones who shine the sunshine
And give the moon its glow

The ones who buff the fluffy clouds
And powder blue the skies
The ones who splash the colours on
The sunset and sunrise

The ones who light volcanoes
The ones who soak the showers
The ones who wave the waves
And open up the flowers

The ones who spring the Spring
And warm the Summer air
The ones who carpet Autumn
And frost the Winter earth

The ones who polish icicles
The ones who scatter stars
The ones who cast their magic spells
Upon this world of ours

Thanks to one and thanks to all
Invisible and true
Nature's magic – heaven sent
To earth for me and you

Figuratively Speaking

If I speak in pictures
Then your ears must be my canvas
And my tongue a brush that paints the words
I want you to imagine

Full of Surprises

This poem is full of surprises
Each line holds something new
This poem is full of surprises
Especially for you . . .

It's full of tigers roaring
It's full of loud guitars
It's full of comets soaring
It's full of shooting stars

It's full of pirates fighting
It's full of winning goals
It's full of alien sightings
It's full of rock and roll

It's full of rainbows beaming
It's full of eagles flying
It's full of dreamers dreaming
It's full of teardrops drying

It's full of magic spells
It's full of wizards' pointy hats
It's full of fairy elves
It's full of witches and black cats

It's full of dragons breathing fire
It's full of dinosaurs
It's full of mountains reaching higher
It's full of warm applause

It's full of everything you need
It's full of more besides
It's full of food, the world to feed
It's full of fairground rides

It's full of love and happiness
It's full of dreams come true
It's full of things that are the best
Especially for you

It's jammed and crammed
And packed and stacked
With things both old and new
This poem is full of surprises
Especially for you

Unique

A crown well worn
Exquisite form
A single ornate silver thorn

The unique horn
The unique horn
The unique horn of the unicorn

The Hummingbird Needs No Words (A Tanka)

Wings that sing rhythms
The hummingbird needs no words
Yet we know its tune
Tune into those good vibrations
Everyday creation song

I Believe in Angels

I believe in angels
Not those who sit on clouds on high
Play harps, have wings that sprout and fly

I believe in angels
Not those who dress in gowns of white
Beneath their halos, gleaming bright

I believe in angels
Not those who live in far-off heaven
But those unknown who we are given

Those who shimmer, those who shine
Who put their own lives last in line

Those whose wings of love enfold us
Those who listen, those who hold us

Those whose wisdom is imparted
Those who heal the broken-hearted

Ordinary angels
Gold that's undiscovered
I believe in angels
Have you met my mother?

My Mother Once Spoke to Judy Garland

My mother once spoke to Judy Garland
Unmoved that she was talking to a star
It must have been the same for Judy Garland
She didn't know just who and what you are

My mother once spoke to Judy Garland
And then she said she'd seen our Auntie Jean
She very rarely mentioned Judy Garland
Very rarely watched the silver screen

Always quiet, always strong
Never said a word that's wrong
Stayed the same all along
Saw the best in everyone
I believe in angels
Ordinary angels

Everything she ever did was for the good of others
Time was just a gift that she could give
Last on any list — just like a lot of mothers
That was just the way she chose to live

Nothing too much trouble, too much bother
The patience of a saint and heaven's grace
No one has a bad word to say of her
Simple and straightforward in her faith

Always quiet, always strong
Never said a word that's wrong
Stayed the same all along
Saw the best in everyone
I believe in angels
Ordinary angels

Judy Garland once spoke to my mother
Two different worlds collide
Two worlds far apart
Hollywood and Lancashire
Rarely meet each other
And she didn't really know
That my mother was the star

Didn't really know
That my mother is the star
One of many shining bright
Glowing in the darkest night
Sign of hope and guiding light
Yes I believe in angels
Ordinary angels

Always quiet, always strong
Never said a word that's wrong
Stayed the same all along
Saw the best in everyone
I believe in angels
Ordinary angels

Take Time to Daydream

Take time to daydream
Look out of every window

Lose yourself in clouds and sky
Drown your imagination in lakes and seas

Entwine yourself in the branches of trees
Hide in caves and darkened shadows

From one solitary grain of sand
To the furthest star

Sit back, reach out, reach out
And take time to daydream

Then dream these daydreams real
One grain of sand at a time

This Poem Needs No Pictures
Save the Ones Inside Your Heart

This poem needs no pictures
Save the ones inside your heart

Let the words sink in
And be a very part of you

May they grow and bloom
Like flowers of the soul

Let them sing their songs
And weave their patterns within you

Carry these verses
Cherish the lines

Learn the meaning
Live and breathe the poetry

These poems need no pictures
Save the ones inside your heart

Come, Embrace the Night
(Adventures in Dreamland)

Come, embrace the night
Come, embrace the dark
This is the time and place
Where new adventures start

The canvas may be black
The canvas blank and deep
New colours will be painted on
Every time we sleep

Welcome every shadow
A gateway is unfurled
Go discover all the other
Secrets from another world

Run free while time is slow
Escape while all are sleeping
Unlock all the riddles
That the nights are keeping

So come, embrace the darkness
Welcome every night
Dreamland and adventures
Until the morning light

Even the Clouds

On a summer's day
When the blue sky page is clearest
Even the clouds spell out your name

In a language only I can understand
I scarce can take it in
Even the clouds spell out your name

They drift and change, shift and fade
God's graffiti, white on blue
Even the clouds spell out your name

A language invisible to all of the others
Signs and wonders, the language of lovers
Even the clouds
Even the clouds
Even the clouds
Spell out your name

Go Explore the Countryside

A summer's day, a bunch of friends
Bows and arrows, building dens
Make believe and let's pretend
All of this and much more when
Finding tallest trees to climb
Leave reality behind
Hide and seek and lots to find
Losing track of space and time
A place to chase and seek and hide
Go explore the countryside

Rope swings over muddy ditches
Stepping stones and building bridges
Snagging clothes on hawthorn hedges
Balancing on stony ledges
Buttercups beneath the chin
Spinning jennies spin and spin
Grass between the thumbs that sing
Dock leaf cures for nettle stings
Hikes to hike and bikes to ride
Go explore the countryside

A piece of penknife poetry
Initialled love hearts there to see
Carved graffiti on the tree
From here to eternity
Flat and smooth skimming stones
Four-leaf clovers, pine cones
Branches look like monster bones
Escape from all the mobile phones
All of these and more beside
Go explore the countryside

Be a cowboy, be a pirate
Let the geography inspire it
Be a soldier, be a knight
Find that stick to fight that fight
Forest shadows, grass that's high
A place to laugh or shout or cry
Caves and bones and stones and rocks
Blowing dandelion clocks
Imagination – far and wide
Go explore the countryside

Let your dog run and run
Lose your dad and hide from Mum
There is space for everyone
In God's fairground filled with fun
Time for families to run wild
Find that hidden inner child

A fallen tree's a crocodile
Lose yourself and stay awhile
Feel the secrets on the breeze
Feel the past within the trees
Eternity in flowing streams
Rugged rocks and crystal seams
In this eternal field of dreams

Go explore, go explore
Go explore – it's what it's for
All of this and much, much more
Mother Nature's superstore
Where geography, biology
And history all collide
There's majesty and mystery
Passing time for me and you
Lots of things to make and do
Yesterdays or something new
Go explore – you know it's true

The magic here, the magic there
Take your time to stop and stare
Be sanctified and goggle-eyed
Satisfied and gratified
Come back to
Come back to
The magic of the countryside

With You, Without You

With you I'm one of the fearless two
Without you I'm the cautious one

With you I think I'm queen of the dance floor
Without you I'm just a clumsy ugly sister

With you my name is complete
Without you it's just waiting for the 'and'

With you I feel a hundred per cent
Without you I'm less than fifty

With you I can take on the world
Without you I just wish that you were here

With you I know that you feel the same
Without you I know that you feel the same too

With you, without you
We are the perfect team

You Get On My Nerves

You get on my nerves
You're a pain in the neck
You drive me to distraction

You can't keep secrets
You can't shut up
That's part of the attraction

You see – you are
Just like me
One after my own heart

You're my best friend
And that is why
I hate it when we are apart

Always . . .

Game playing
Secret sharing
Loud laughing – friends

Bike riding
Book reading
TV watching – friends

Sweet eating
Crazy dancing
Always talking – friends

Unspoken

Inspired by Stephen King

Someone once wrote
'I never had friends later on
Like the ones I had when I was twelve'
And not for the first time . . . he was right

You know you'd do anything for them
The friends you'd make a stand for
Lie for and fight for
The ones who know your secrets
And your deepest fears
The only ones who can joke about them
And get away with it
Those who call you the worst names ever
And insult your whole family
In varied and interesting ways . . .
All with a smile
But then turn on others who do the same

Invisible – but ever present
More than just loyalty
It was the word that was never mentioned
The word that was always there

Unspoken

The Day the Rope Swing Broke

I'm glad that it was not my go
High and low and to and fro
Above the water down below
The day the rope swing broke

I'm glad that I was high and dry
I'd be a liar to deny
I laughed enough to make me cry
The day the rope swing broke

I'm so glad he was the one
Much too heavy to get on
A moment later he was gone
The day the rope swing broke

A rush of air and then a splatter
Feel the mud and water scatter
It serves Dad right for being fatter
The day the rope swing broke

Dad Don't Dab

Dad don't dab
Dad don't dab
The bad dab bad dad dance

Dab like Dad
Drive Mum mad
Look really sad
When you dab like Dad

Dad don't dab in the doorway
Dad don't dab in the drive way
Dad don't dab on the dishwasher
Dad don't dab on the dog!

Dad don't dab on your dinner
Dad don't dab in the dryer
Dad don't drink and dab
Dad don't drive and dab

Dad don't dab
Dad don't dab
The bad dad bad dad bad dad bad dad
Bad dad bad dab dance

These Are the Hands

These are the hands that wave
These are the hands that clap
These are the hands that pray
These are the hands that tap

These are the hands that grip
These are the hands that write
These are the hands that paint
These are the hands that fight

These are the hands that hug
These are the hands that squeeze
These are the hands that point
These are the hands that tease

These are the hands that take
These are the hands that poke
These are the hands that give
These are the hands that stroke

These are the hands that hold
These are the hands that love
These two hands of ours
They fit us like a glove

I Would Win the Gold
If These Were Olympic Sports . . .

Bubble gum blowing
Goggle box watching
Late morning snoring
Homework botching

Quilt ruffling
Little brother teasing
Pizza demolishing
Big toe cheesing

Insult hurling, wobbly throwing
Infinite blue belly button fluff growing

Late night endurance computer screen gazing
Non-attentive open-jawed eyeball glazing

Ultimate volume decibel blaring
Long distance marathon same sock wearing

Recognize all these as sports, then meet . . .
Me! The Champ Apathetic Athlete!

An Alphabet of Alphabeastical Facts You Didn't Know You Knew

Ants cannot play tubas
Bats cannot hit cricket balls
Crocodiles can't rock and roll
Dolphins can't climb walls

Emus can't do DIY
Flies can't ride a bike
Gnus can't read the TV news
Horses cannot write

Iguanas cannot rollerskate
Jaguars can't play guitars
Kangaroos can't conga
Llamas can't drive cars

Monkeys can't do crosswords
Newts can't play trombones
Orang-utans can't deep sea dive
Penguins can't use mobile phones

Quala Bears can't spell
Rhinos cannot tightrope walk
Squids cannot climb trees
Tarantulas can't squawk

Unicorns can't belly dance
Vipers cannot ski
Wombats cannot ice skate
Xtinct things can't be

Yetis can't be spotted
Zebras can't turn blue
All these amazing facts
You didn't know you knew

All these amazing facts
Especially for you
An alphabet of facts
And all of them are true

Crazy at the Zoo

There's a penguin eating pizza
A lion in the loo
A bear that wears pink underwear
It's crazy at the zoo

A rock and rolling rhino
A kung fu kangaroo
A hip hop hippopotamus
It's crazy at the zoo

A ballet dancing buffalo
In a tiny tutu too
An elephant in spotty pants
It's crazy at the zoo

The zebra's stripes are painted
Orange, red and blue
The tiger's pink and purple
It's crazy at the zoo

A gecko with an echo
Is g-nagging the gnu
A giggling gorilla
It's crazy at the zoo

A parrot that is potty
Sings Cock-a-doodle-doo
A crocodile with a toothless smile
It's crazy at the zoo

Monkeys wearing lipstick
Bonkers but it's true
Snakes in socks are tied in knots
It's crazy at the zoo

An orang-utan that tangoes
With a cockatoo
A sloth that coughs and races off
It's crazy at the zoo

All the clever keepers
Know just what to do
They're selling lots of tickets
Lots and lots of tickets
Selling lots more tickets
Now it's crazy – at – the zoo!

Stormy Promise Haiku

The rainbow after
God's graffiti does make it
Easy to believe

The Shortest Day of the Year

Lazy sun
Clocks in late
Clocks off early
If at all

Haik-ewe

Sheep in the distance
Are small clouds on the hillside
Nimbus flocks and flecks

Jack Frost

Jack Frost
Winter wizard
Brightens up the darkest night
Spells while we are fast asleep

Jack Frost
Winter jeweller
Encrusting webs with diamonds
Icicle fingertips, silver breath

Jack Frost
Winter graffiti artist
Spray-can magic leaves its mark
Christmas card scenery, the icing on the cake

The Last Day of Summer

Shadows lengthen one last time
Ice-cream vans hibernate
Shorts are banished to the bottom drawer
Cricket bats and tennis racquets go back to being
Pretend guitars and machine guns
Barbecues burn sausages no more
Shirtsleeves roll down, not up
And somewhere beneath the stairs
There is the rustling of warmer coats
As woollen gloves gently wake from slumber
Deep inside their padded nests

The First Snow of Winter

Waking up to the scrunching carpet crunch
The photographic negative
Cotton wool icing
The transforming blanket
Where even city centres
Could be picture Christmas cards
Every child delves in the understairs cupboard
for winter coats and wellington boots
Wanting to be the first
The very first, the very, very first
To leave their mark, their own print
And hear the sound of footprints in the snow

Stairway to the Clouds

I took a stairway to the clouds
And a camel to the moon
A trampoline to Timbuktu
A rocket to my room

A skateboard to the Red Sea
A submarine to Mars
A freight train to Atlantis
I dived up to the stars

Parachuting on the ocean
I rode my bike down deep
I took a racing car to bed
And drove myself to sleep

I caught a bus that flew
To a bridge across the seas
And then in my canoe
I slalomed through the trees

I scootered on thin ice
Space-hopped into space
With ice skates on the running track
I raced the human race

I bounced upon my pogo stick
All round the equator
I scaled the peak of Everest
Thanks to an elevator

I rope swing through the cities
Piggyback through towns
Ride horses down the rivers
Ski deep down underground

I swim across the deserts
Surf on escalators
Rollerskate on glaciers
Leapfrog high skyscrapers

I've travelled many places
In many different styles
Near and far and deep and wide
Millions of miles

No matter how I wander
No matter where I roam
Of all these special journeys
The best one is . . . back home

First and Lasting Impressions

I want to be

The first shadow dancing on the sunrise
The last negative ghost that lengthens into darkness

The first footprint crump crump
On the blank and silent snowy canvas
The last drop that melts
Disappearing into sunlight

The first explosive splash
Shattering the mirrored pool
The last slowing ripple
Ironed into calmness

The first track on the ocean-swept beach
The last print washed into watery oblivion

First and lasting impressions

We Saw Stars

Some saw only shadows
While we saw only light
Some saw only darkness
While we embraced the night
Some saw midnight blackness
While we saw comets bright

We believe in rainbows
Dreams and shooting stars
We believe the future
We believe the future
We believe the future
Will be ours

The Trees Whisper their Secrets on the Wind

The trees whisper their secrets on the wind

If you listen carefully
Closely, carefully and silently
You may catch them

Tune your heart
Attune your ears
For what these trees can tell you

Silent guardians, arms outstretched
All are welcome beneath their boughs

Times and places
Childhood games

Secret lovers
Midnight trysts

Innocent confessions
Lonely tears

New adventures
Great journeys

Fresh starts
Heartfelt prayers

Promises made in the witness
Of oak and sycamore and chestnut and pine

The secrets soaked into their bark
Draw near and hold their history close
Feel the past beneath your fingers

And listen, listen . . . listen
For that moment when the trees
Will whisper their secrets upon the wind

Poets are Photographers

Poets are photographers
Capturing moments in words

Snapshots of humanity
Pinpoints of reality

Poets are photographers
Capturing images in language

Articulators of feelings
Mirrors of experience

Poets are photographers
Capturing emotions on pages

Seekers of the common ground
Sharers of the everyday

Poets are photographers
Capturing the elusive

Scribes of the wondrous
Chroniclers of the mundane

Poets are photographers
Poems are their pictures

Remembering Is Our Duty

Let no one take the memories we cherish
Let no one break the cycle of remembrance
The trivial, the everyday
These fragments that make up our lives
Let no one taint the memories we cherish

Let's celebrate the art of not forgetting
Let's celebrate the art of total recall
The past that makes our present
The present that's our future
Let's celebrate the art of not forgetting

The Poppy Red – Lest Ever We Forget

This century on and still we shall recall
With heart and soul we now salute you all
And recognize those lives that went before
And pray that peace may conquer any war

Bravery we cannot comprehend
Passing time does not the sorrow mend
Battles that we do not understand
We pray there's no return to No Man's Land
The heroes that we never met
The poppy red – lest ever we forget

Those memories forever will remain
We pray will not tread that path again
Too many lost so we may live
Remembrance – all that we can give
We never can repay that debt
The poppy red – lest ever we forget

On Flanders Fields, the trenches and Dunkirk
When evil hums then good must do its work
Their sacrifice lives on eternally
Their inspiration and their dignity
Dulce et decorum est
The poppy red – lest ever we forget

This century on and still we shall recall
With heart and soul we now salute you all
And recognize those lives that went before
And pray that peace may conquer any war
So let us join as one and pay respect
The poppy red – lest ever we forget

Just for Another Minute

On the eleventh of the eleventh
At eleven o'clock
We all stopped

We all stopped doing maths,
Put our pens down
And closed our eyes for a minute

A whole minute

At first I wanted to work on the answer
To the question I was stuck on,
Then I wanted to think about football . . .
But I couldn't, I just couldn't

The silence made me think about poppies
And the old men in medals who sold them
Down the shopping centre

The old men with walking sticks
Who once carried guns
And fought in a war I could not understand
A real war, not like on the videos

And even though I didn't know anyone like that
I was a sad, just a little bit sad

Before I knew it the minute was over
And the silence was gone
But I wanted it to carry on,
I wanted to carry on thinking,
I wanted the silence again

Just for another minute

Donald Simpson Bell

From football to the front line
From the pitch to No Man's Land
From shots at goals to bullet holes
From goals to all posts manned
Beyond the call of duty
The dangers that he knew so well
Victoria Cross – war and loss
Donald Simpson Bell

Instead of cups and trophies
This, his legacy
The only working footballer
To win it for his bravery
Not exploits on the football field
But in that living hell
Victoria Cross – war and loss
Donald Simpson Bell

July the fifth, 1916
The Battle of the Somme
His story became history
That strike in World War One
Dodging heavy German fire
Each bullet, bomb and shell
Victoria Cross – war and loss
Donald Simpson Bell

That bomb that hit its target true
That saved those fifty lives
Gallantry and bravery
His legacy survives
Alas then, five days later
This story, sad to tell
Victoria Cross – war and loss
Donald Simpson Bell

Another one cut down too soon
Another in his prime
Another fallen hero
Gone before his time
But Bell's Redoubt – the monument
To mark the place he fell
Victoria Cross – war and loss
Donald Simpson Bell

Love, Hope and Strength

For Mike and Jules Peters

May the love of those around you
Enfold you in its wings
May the hope of those uplift you
Time and time again
May all those who surround you
Give you strength within

May the prayers of those who pray for you
Be answered from the start
May the light of those both near and far
Shine amidst the dark
May the fellowship of friends
Be forever in your heart

May the love and hope and strength and light
Ease your heavy load
May all of this and much, much more
Support you all along the road

May the arms of those who hold you
Carry you along
May the tongues of those who sing
Forever sing your song
May the hearts of those who love you
Keep you ever strong

May the eyes of those who look out
See you through each day
May the ears of those who listen
Hear each word you say
May the laughter and the smiles
Illuminate each shadowed way

May the love and hope and strength and light
Ease your heavy load
May all of this and much, much more
Carry you much further down the road

Five Sense-able Haikus

TASTE

Twisty tangy zest
Lime and lemon ice cream to
Twizzle on my tongue

SMELL

Fish, chips, vinegar
Freshly baked bread, new mown grass
My nose knows no bounds

TOUCH

Nettle sting, cold ice
Hot stove, burnt fingers – not nice
Touch it once – not twice!

SIGHT

Pure sky, pastel blue
Ocean green, rose red, snow white
Four favourite sights

SOUND

When Grandma giggles
As Grandad's stomach gurgles
Music to my ears

Raining on the Trip

It's raining on the trip
Raining on the trip
Drip drip drip
Raining on the trip

It's never going to stop
Never going to stop
Drop drop drop
Never going to stop

I haven't got a coat
Haven't got a coat
Splish splash splosh
Going to get soaked

I think it's going to flood
Think it's going to flood
Thud thud thud
Think it's going to flood

The clouds are getting dark
Clouds are getting dark
Any more rain
We're going to need an ark

It's raining on the trip
Raining on the trip
Drip drip drip
Raining on the trip

It's never going to stop
Never going to stop
Drop drop drop
Never going to stop

Drop drop drop
Never going to stop
Drop drop drop
Never going to . . .

Just Mum and Me

We didn't do anything special today,
just Mum and me.
Raining outside, nowhere to go,
just Mum and me.

So we baked and talked and talked and baked
and baked and talked,
just Mum and me.

She told me about when she was young
and how her gran baked exactly the same cakes
on rainy days and baked and talked to her.

She remembers her friends
and the games they used to play,
the trees they used to climb
the fields they used to run around in
and how summers always seemed to be sunny.

And Mum smiled a smile I don't often see,
the years falling away from her face,
and just for a moment
I caught a glimpse of the girl she used to be.

We didn't do anything special today,
raining outside, nowhere to go,
so we baked and talked and talked and baked,
just Mum and me.

I ate and listened and listened and ate,
the hours racing by so quickly.

We didn't do anything special . . .
but it was special, really special.

Just Mum and me.

Father's Hands

Father's hands
Large like frying pans
Broad as shovel blades
Strong as weathered spades

Father's hands
Finger ends ingrained with dirt
Permanently stained from work
Ignoring pain and scorning hurt

I once saw him walk boldly
up to a swan that had landed
in next door's drive and wouldn't move.
The police were there because
swans are a protected species
but didn't do anything
but my dad walked up to it,
picked it up and carried it away.
No problem.
Those massive wings
that can break a man's bones
were held tight, tight by my father's hands
and I was proud of him that day.
Really proud

Father's hands
Tough as leather on old boots
Firmly grasping nettle shoots
Pulling thistles by their roots

Father's hands
Gripping like an iron vice
Never numb in snow or ice
Nails and screws are pulled and prised

He once found a kestrel with a broken wing
and kept it in our garage until it was better
He'd feed it by hand
with scraps of meat or dead mice
and you could tell where its beak and talons
had taken bits from his finger ends.
It never seemed to hurt him it all,
he just smiled
as he let it claw and peck

Father's hands
Lifting bales of hay and straw
Callused, hardened, rough and raw
Building, planting, painting, more . . .

Father's hands
Hard when tanning my backside
All we needed they supplied
And still my hands will fit inside

Father's hands
Large like frying pans
Broad as shovel blades
Strong as weathered spades

And still my hands will fit inside
My father's hands.

The Big Shed

A ramshackle den of clutter,
A mazy mixture of the useful and the useless,
The rubbish, the rusty, the wood and the mud.

At least three small sheds' worth
Of tongue and groove and four by two,
Dismantled and flat packed . . . well, sort of . . .
All jumbled zig-zag seesaw heaps.

The monster orange rotavator,
Its giant teeth caked with mud
Silent and untamed
I was never allowed to grapple this beast
Until I was at secondary school.

The dead red and white motor scooter
Complete with windshield and crash helmet
That Dad could never get to work
But Cousin Paul took and resurrected.

Stacks and stacks and stacks
Of multi-purpose bamboo canes
That would become arrows, guns or swords
Depending on last night's television.

Hay bales, musty, dusty and precarious
Transformed into cowboy forts, mountains,
Castles or sheer rock faces
Depending on last night's television.

The bowed wooden barrel we broke
One Summer holiday afternoon
When trying to walk inside it
The barrel over our heads
Because we were re-enacting an adventure
From *Scooby Doo*.

The legend of 'Hairy Face'
Created then extended
From nothing to belief
Thanks to invented sightings
And pretend happenings
All scratchings, creakings and whistlings
Became his.
No one really believed in 'Hairy Face'
Until they were left alone at dusk
When darkness extended its bony fingers
Squeezing out remaining light
And then 'Hairy Face' lurked
In every single shadow.

Hide-and-seek became a game
With endless possibilities
No two games identical
Our options knew few limits
As plastic sheets, piles of planks,
Pallets and potato sacks
Chimney pots and high haystacks
Were rearranged to conceal us that little bit longer.

We could lose ourselves for hours
In this ramshackle den of clutter,
That mazy mixture of the rubbish and the rusty
The wood, the mud, the useful, the useless
And us.

Dad's Whiskery Kiss

Matchbox chin
Sandpaper lips
Barbed wire jaw
Whiskery kiss

Cactus skin
Brillo pad thistle
Nettle rash neck
Prickly bristle

Hedgehog scrape
Porcupine twist
That's my dad's
Whiskery kiss

There's no way
You can resist
Dad's unshaven
Whiskery kiss

Mum and Dad are Mum and Dad

Mum and Dad are Mum and Dad
Well, they are — but in some ways they're not
You see, although they didn't actually
Physically bring me into this world
They did bring me up in this world

Adopted at birth
Mum and Dad are Mum and Dad
And always have been

Never once have I wanted to go back
Trace the roots and dig up the past
Never once have I wanted to question
Face to face and flesh to flesh
With whoever brought me into this world
And then, for whatever reason
Let me go

What has been is
What will be is
What is is
And never once have I wanted to change it

Mum and Dad are Mum and Dad
Always have been
And always will be

They chose me
And if I had a choice
I know with all my heart
That I could not have chosen better

The Planet where the Lost Things Go

The single sock from the washing machine
The last teaspoon that's never seen
Remote controls for DVDs
Mum's hair brush and Dad's car keys
There's one place you'll find all these
The planet of the lost

A phone number on a Post-it note
A single glove from a winter coat
The lottery ticket that should have won
Unfinished poems, unsung songs
We all know where they have gone
The planet of the lost

The concert ticket – not attended
The novel started – never ended
Love letters – never sent
Foreign coins – left unspent
Can you guess where they all went?
The planet of the lost

Magically magnetized
Beyond the earth and clouds and skies
Dissolved into the atmosphere
Thin air as they reappear
Safe and sound now they're all here
The planet of the lost

Constellations

Grandad would often look up to the stars
From our back garden
Looking up to the dark night sky
Pointing out the patterns and constellations . . .

The Plough, The Great Bear, Orion's Belt

I could never see them and make them out
Neither could Dad
He would look up, point at them
And make different pictures

God's Big Pants
A Sock for a Giant Squid
The Sausage Strings of Saturn

And my own personal favourite . . .

The toilet from outer space

6 November – Last Night's Life

Last night's magic, last night's colours
Last night's sparkle, last night's fizz
Last night's snap, last night's crackle
Last night's pop, last night's whizz

Last night's boom, last night's crash
Last night's bangs today are found
Blackened, ash-stained, shattered cardboard
Dead and scattered on the ground

The Day We Built the Snowman

Round and round the garden,
Rolling up the snow,
One step, two step,
Watch the snowman grow.

Round and round the garden,
Us and Dad and Mum,
Building up the snowman,
Having lots of fun.

Mum has got a carrot,
Dad has got a pipe,
Sister's got a scarf
To keep him warm at night.

Baseball cap and shades,
Trainers for his feet,
Our trendy friendly snowman,
The coolest in the street.

Round and round the garden
In the winter weather
The day we built the snowman . . .
Having fun together.

Round and round the garden,
Rolling up the snow,
One step, two step,
Watch the snowman grow.

Round and round the garden,
Us and Dad and Mum,
Building up the snowman,
Having lots of fun.

Stay Away From the Manger

To the tune of 'Away in a Manger'

Stay away from the manger
Is what teacher said
Last year our Lord Jesus
Was dropped on his head
So Mary hit Joseph
Who then tripped a sheep
The shepherds and wise men
Fell down in a heap

The donkey fell over
And rolled off the stage
On to the piano
As Miss turned the page
The lid on her fingers
Came down with a CRACK!
The words that she shouted
Were heard at the back

So this year the infants
Are not in the show
We all said 'Pleeeaaassse'
But teacher said no
Stay away from the manger
You're not going to spoil it
By waving at parents
And wanting the toilet

I Wish I'd Been Present at Christmas Past

I wish I'd been a shepherd
And heard the angels sing.
I wish I'd been to Bethlehem
And seen the Infant King.

I wish I'd been a wise man
At the stable bare
Following the star with
Gold, frankincense and myrrh.

I wish I'd been an animal
Who shared my manger hay
With that special newborn baby
On the first Christmas Day.

Too Excited

Tonight I'm too excited
To try and get to sleep
Mum and Dad have told me
To try by counting sheep
Instead I'm counting reindeer
Their noses glowing red
Each one I count just makes me
More wide awake instead
The more I count, the closer
Santa seems to be
And I just love the magic
And the mystery

This Year I Will Stay Awake

This year I will stay awake
all night long, make no mistake.
On this Christmas Eve I'll keep
my eyes open, try to peep.
This year I won't drowse or dream
but be alert till Santa's been,
see just what he leaves and how
he fits down our chimney now,
how the presents all appear
hear the sleigh bells and reindeer.
This year I will not count sheep
but pretend to be asleep.
No catnaps or snoozing but I
won't drop off and get some shut-eye.

This year there will be no slumber
I won't let myself go under.
No forty winks or throwing zeds.
No blinking, kipping, heavy headszz . . .
This year I won't nod or doze
or let my heavy eyelids close.
This year I won't nod or doze
or let my heavy eyelids close
or let my heavy eyelids close
or let my he..avy eye..li..ds clo..se
or let my he..avy eye..liiids clo..zzzzzzzzzzzzzzz

Take Note

I emailed Father Christmas
At santaclaus.com
With this year's Christmas list
And everything I want
Expensive and expansive
I asked for such a lot
Then Santa emailed back
And this is what I got:
A print-out of another list
Of things that I should leave
At the bottom of the chimney
On this Christmas Eve . . .
Snow-proof leather wellingtons
Thermal underwear
Gloves with fleecy lining
A hat that's lined with fur
A scarf that's extra extra long
To wrap around a beard of white
Goggles for the snowstorms
Headlights for the darkest night
Reindeer socks and woolly hats
Carrots, milk and oats
Sherry, pies and whisky
To warm up winter throats
Chocolate bars for energy

Coffee, tea and cake
Matchsticks to help tired eyes
To try and stay awake
It finished with a little note
From Santa Claus himself
Wishing us the very best
Happiness and health
I read it once, then once again –
Seeing is believing –
He said, 'Remember, Christmas is
For giving, not receiving'

The Day After the Day
After Boxing Day

On the day after the day after Boxing Day
Santa wakes up . . . eventually
Puts the big red suit in the wash
Cleans the wellington boots
Lets Rudolph and the gang out into the meadow
Then shaves his head and beard

He puts on his new sunglasses
Baggy blue holiday shorts (he's sick of red)
Yellow stripy T-shirt
That doesn't quite stretch over his belly
And lets his toes breathe in flip-flops

Packing a bucket and spade
Fifteen tubes of high-factor sun cream
Twenty page-turning holiday reads
Downloads his favourite songs on the new iPod
And is glad to use a suitcase instead of the sack
As he heads off to an island in the sun

Six months later
Totally relaxed and more than a little stubbly
He looks at his watch
Adjusts his sun hat
Mops the sweat from his brow
Strokes the new beard
And wonders why holidays
Always seem to go so quickly

Ho ho hum, he thinks
Back to work
Tomorrow

Open a Book

Open a book and you open the world
Open a new book – you find a new world
A world within worlds
Within words within words
Taste the freedom of adventure
Run wild, run wild, run wild

Open a book and you open your mind
Close a book and you close your mind
Unlock the secrets, embrace the magic
Let each turning page
Colour imagination

Run free, run wild, run wild and free with
New friends to love and cherish
New friends to share experiences with
New friends to teach you

Learn from their stories
Learn from their lives
Learn from their mistakes
Learn from their loves

No one is ever freed by grammar
Subjunctive clauses, prepositions, suffixes,
Fronted adverbials would only be exciting
If they were monsters to escape from . . .
Which indeed they are

But stories . . . aah, stories . . .
Stories free our hearts and minds
The confines of the pages
Are universes to explore

No one has ever needed a semicolon
But a good story is a friend forever
So run free, run free
Revel in these stories
Dance along to their music
Sing the adventures
Cry the emotions
Laugh the danger away

All life is here
There is joy in them there pages
A good story is a friend for ever and ever
Amen

Football Has It All

History and legacy
Champions and trophies
Heroes and villains
Football has it all

For the people by the people
Universal language
Truly international
Football has it all

The World Cup in the playground
Wembley in our gardens
Premier League in every park
Football has it all

Memories to cherish
When all time stood still
The bookmarks of our lives
Football has it all

So much we can learn from
So much it can teach us
So very many dreams
Football has it all

It's a Game of Numbers

Four four two
Three five three
Eleven vee eleven

Three o'clock
Ninety minutes
Forty-five each way

Three points, one point, zero
Score one more than them
It's a game of numbers

Front two
Flat back four
Big number nine

Fifty thousand cheering
Hundred grand a week
Multimillionaires

Four two
Number one
Nineteen sixty-six

It's a game of numbers

Football Counting Rhyme

I kicked my ball
Once against the wall
Twice in the bathroom
Three times in the hall

4 – in the kitchen
5 – at the door
6 – at my sister
Seven times more

8 – against the gate
9 – against the slide
10 – at the greenhouse
Then I had to hide!

11 – in the driveway
12 – on my bed
13 – at the garage
14 – at the shed

15 – at the dog
16 – at the cat
17 – at my granny
Knocking off her hat

18 – in the kitchen
19 – on the grass
20 – at the window
Breaking all the glass!

Poem for the First Day of the Football Season

Brand-new start,
last season is history and meaningless.

My team has no points
and neither has yours.

All things are possible
and all glory dreamable.

Everything is winnable
Potential is unmissable.

The peak of faith is scaleable
The mountain of hope is touchable
The summit of belief, believable.

Ten to three on that first Saturday
and nothing dulls the taste.

Excitement and anticipation
tangible and tasteable.

Unparalleled success attainable
this could be the best season of our lives.

Poem for the Last Day of the Football Season

Dreams in tatters
Hopes in rags
Blown away
Like paper bags

Early exits
From each cup
My team down
Your team up

Shadows lengthen
The worst I fear
But I'll be back
Same time next year

Home

It's who we are
It's what we do
It's why we're here
It's me and you
It's where we laugh
It's where we cry
And where we shout and gasp and groan
It's where we meet
Week by week
Everton – at home
Everton – at home

At home with those who care
At home with those who dare to dream
More than just a football crowd
More than just a football team

It's church and it's belonging
Weekly mass – communion
It's faith and hope and love and more
It's family, friends, our union

At home we know our places
The special points where we all meet
And all the usual faces
The click-clack of a myriad seats

That music before kick-off
That heralds expectation
The *Z Cars* theme, a Grand Old Team
Excitement and anticipation

Not just what happens on the pitch
Those in blue on Goodison green
Important landmarks of our lives
Marked by matches we've all seen

Guardians of tradition
We pass that baton on
The heroes of the past
The heroes yet to come

Those magic moments that we shared
The joy and pain we've known
It's where we meet – week by week
Everton – at home

The guiding lights on winter's nights
The Grand Old Lady's throne
It's where we meet – week by week
Everton – at home

Born not manufactured
Never on your own
It's where we meet – week by week
Everton – at home

It's who we are
It's what we do
It's why we're here
It's me and you
It's where we pray – on Saturday
For future hopes unknown
Our history and legacy
Those times to come for you and me
It's where we meet
Week by week
Everton – at home
Everton – at home

Oh Glory Be

Inspired by Kate Rusby

Oh glory be to all the songs
Salvation songs of truth
Those passed down through history
That we learned in our youth
Oh glory be to all the songs
The ballads, reels and rhyme
Hymns and carols we all know
That stand the test of time

Oh glory be to all the songs
Honest, good and true
Songs of laughter, songs of tears
Old but ever new
Oh glory be to all the songs
That lighten up the dark
Chart those feelings we all feel
And map the human heart

Sweet chiming songs – sweet chiming songs
Oh blessed chiming songs

Oh glory be to all the songs
And everything they bring
All the songs with open arms
That welcome all within
Oh glory be to all the songs
That span both time and age
With one foot with the people
And one foot on the stage

Sweet chiming songs – sweet chiming songs
Oh blessed chiming songs

Oh glory be to all the songs
Each cadent melody
Entwines itself within our lives
With heavenly mystery
Oh glory to bc to all the songs
Each perfect in thcir way
Who capture in their majesty
Those things we cannot say

Sweet chiming songs – sweet chiming songs
Oh blessed chiming songs

We Are the Writers

For Longhill Primary School

We are readers, we are writers
We love to share the words that excite us

We are poets, we are singers
We love to share the melodies they bring us

We are actors, we are dancers
We love to have the questions and the answers

It only takes one spark to start the fire
Just one idea to inspire
It only takes one dream to take you higher

It only takes one voice to breathe these words
So they live and so they can be heard
These lines and these rhymes will give the world
So many writers

We are searchers, we are seekers
Where there are secrets, we are the keepers

We are doers, we are makers
We are the movers, we are the shakers

We are thinkers, we are dreamers
We are here because we are believers . . .

It only takes one spark to start the fire
Just one idea to inspire
It only takes one dream to take you higher

It only takes one voice to breathe these words
So they live and so they can be heard
These lines and these rhymes will give the world
So many writers

We are readers, we are writers
We love to share the words that excite us

We are the writers

*Paul Cookson, Stan Cullimore
and Henry Priestman*

Every Child Likes Acrostics Because . . .

Poems that children like writing best are
Acrostics because you can look down the
Next line and guess
The word that is being
Spelled down the left-hand side

There's a Big Bad Bug in my Lunch Box

There's a big bad bug in my lunch box
I don't know what to do
It's eaten up my sandwiches
My chocolate biscuits too

There's a big bad bug in my lunch box
All legs and shiny claws
Bits of my jam doughnut
Are hanging from its jaws

There's a big bad bug in my lunch box
And now it's time for lunch
So . . . I picked it, bit it, ate it up
CRUNCH! CRUNCH! CRUNCH!

This is Our School

This is our school
These are our friends
The journey that starts here
Will never end

This is our school
A place where we can grow
Where teachers can teach us
Things we need to know

Here we learn to read and write
Here we learn to share and play
Here we learn together
Day by day, day by day

Here we learn all the lessons
That will help us on our way
Through the years, we are here
Day by day, day by day

This is our school
For you and for me
A place we can wish
A place we can dream

This is our school
Full of memories
Classrooms of knowledge
And discovery

Here we learn to read and write
Here we learn to share and play
Here we learn together
Day by day, day by day

Here we learn all the lessons
That will help us on our way
Through the years, we are here
Day by day, day by day

The days they turn to weeks
The weeks they turn to years
We may pass on through
But our school is always here

This is our school
More than these walls
We are the school
For one and for all

Paul Cookson, Stan Cullimore
and Henry Priestman

Dear Head Teacher . . .

I'm writing to say sorry
About your window that was smashed
It wasn't me that did it . . .
But someone from my class

I did not kick the ball
I didn't really know
I didn't see the shot that took it
Through your new window . . .

I wasn't even playing
I just happened to be standing
And didn't have a clue
Where the ball would end up landing

I wasn't really looking
As my eyes were closed instead
It wasn't my fault
When the ball bounced off my head

If it hadn't hit my head
It would just have hit the wall
But you're the one
Who told me to be standing there at all

Everybody laughed
At the ricochet deflection
Well . . . everyone but me
When the football changed direction

Everyone said 'Smashing!'
And 'Oooh what a beauty!'
But it wasn't my fault . . .

I was just on playground duty

All Teachers Great and Small

Mrs Bright is beautiful
Mr Short is seven feet tall
Mr Cullimore's a bore
All teachers great and small

Mrs Priest's a scary beast
Mr Hall looks likes a ball
Mr Shepherd's sheepish
All teachers great and small

Miss O'Rourke is from New York
'Hi, y'all,' she'll drawl
Mr Whyatt's oh so quiet
All teachers great and small

Mrs Pride always arrives
Just before Mr Fall
Miss Glover knows that we all love her
All teachers great and small

Mr, Miss and Mrs
All teachers great and small
Wise and weird and wonderful
The Lord God made them all

Teacher

Loud shouter
Deep thinker
Rain hater
Coffee drinker

Spell checker
Sum ticker
Line giver
Nit picker

Ready listener
Trouble carer
Hometime lover
Knowledge sharer

It's Not the Same Any More

It's not the same any more
Sticks are just sticks
Never thrown, never fetched

It's not the same any more
Tennis balls lie still and lifeless
The urge to bounce them has gone

It's not the same now
I can't bring myself to whistle
There's no reason to do so

His collar hangs on the hook
The name tag and lead are dusty

His basket and bowl are in a plastic bag
Lying at an awkward angle on the garage shelf

My new slippers will never be chewed
And I've no excuse
For lack of homework any more

The football can be watched uninterrupted
No frantic barking and leaping about
Just as it gets to the goal

I don't have to share biscuits
Or wipe drool from my trouser legs

It's just not the same any more
When Patch died, a small part of me died too

All that's left is the mound of earth
And my handmade cross beneath the apple tree

All that's left are the memories
Thousands of them

It's just not the same any more

The Rattlesnake Shake

The rattlesnake shake
Rattlesnake shake
Shake shake shake
The rattlesnake shake

You can slither and shiver
You can quiver and quake
Smooth as a river
Still as a lake
Still as a lake

You can slip and slide
Swing and sway
Siide to sssiiiide
Night and day
Come what may

Let the coils uncoil
Scales shine bright
Slick like oil
Fast as light
Dark as night

You can twist and turn
Mesmeriiiiize
Squeeze and squirm
Hypnotiiiiiize

The rattlesnake shake
Rattlesnake shake
Shake shake shake
The rattlesnake shake

Shake shake shake
The rattlesnake . . . shake

Beware of The Grey

Beware of The Grey
Beware of The Grey
Fading your dreams
And ambitions away

Beware of The Grey
Beware of The Grey
Melting the night time
Into the day

He'll take all your colours
And drain them away
Beware of the evil
Beware of The Grey

Whatever you do
Whatever you say
Keep your eyes open
Beware of The Grey

Don't put off tomorrow
What can be today
Follow your vision
Beware of The Grey

He'll shade all your dreams
Whisper and say
'Don't worry – give up'
Beware of The Grey

Where there's a will
There's always a way
Little by little
Beware of The Grey

He'll suck out your energy
Say it's OK
To accept second best
Beware of The Grey

Beware of The Grey
Beware of The Grey
Fading your dreams
And ambitions away

Honour Your Place of Silence

Wherever there is silence
There is thoughtfulness and contemplation
Where there is contemplation
There is often meditation and prayer

Whoever it is you pray to
And we all do from time to time
Wherever and however you pray these prayers
In doing so

Honour your place of silence
Honour your meditations
Honour your own prayerfulness
For in doing so

You honour the silence
And prayerfulness of others
For they do that to you
Amen

The Gifts We Do Not Give

You have the gift of peace
So why do you give conflict?

You have the gift of love
So why do you give hate?

You have the gift of laughter
So why do you give tears?

You have the gift of joy
So why do you give hurt?

Forgiveness is Out of Fashion

Forgiveness seems out of fashion
Sorry seems to be an act of weakness
Not accepting those who disagree
Or those we do not understand
Or those we simply do not like
Is now the everyday

Forgiveness seems out of fashion
It is an act we need to learn
A habit we need to practise
A muscle we need to exercise
And a shirt we need to wear
Every day

And most of all
We must learn to be unfashionable

The Greatest Message

Embrace this feeling we call faith
Believe and live in hope and truth
Learn to love as we'd be loved
The idealism of our youth

It's time to banish all those schemes
That would invade and sour our dreams
It's time to stand and turn our backs
On all the forces that attack

It's time to act, it's time to face
The powers that erode our faith
The faith passed down that we inherit
The strength within the human spirit

It's time to see through grown-up eyes
Once and for all to realize
That love is love is love is love
And nothing to be frightened of

Yes, love is love is love is love
Like black and white, like hand in glove
Patient, kind and from above
Yes love is love is love is love

So keep the faith, hold tight the hope
Hope for the future we dream of
Faith, hope and love, these three remain
The greatest of them all is love

Man's Best Friend

He's not a bad pet really . . .
I've had him years now
I've got used to his ways
I suppose he's got used to mine as well.

He's not as young as he used to be . . .
His eyesight's going
And sometimes he can be a bit deaf.
When he wants to be!

He's put on some extra weight too . . .
I take him for walks but
They're shorter, less frequent these days.
He's not as energetic as he once was.

We don't really play any games now . . .
He can't catch the frisbee any more,
Sticks are left alone and when the football burst
There didn't seem much point in buying another.

He sleeps most of the time . . .
Seems to like it by the fire best these days
With a warm tartan rug
And the comforting sound of the television.

Occasionally he perks up a bit . . .
Especially if it involves chocolate,
Homemade ginger cake from Mrs B next door
Or a visit from the grandchildren.

But mostly it's like this . . .
Peaceful
Comfortable
Friendly.

We look after each other these days . . .
I trust him with my life.
Best friends, I wouldn't swap him for anything.
We've seen some things!

Yes, he's the best master any dog could wish for.

The Happiest Man with the Happiest Dog at the Happiest Time of the Day

The stress and strain of a working life
Weigh heavy day by day
But when I'm walking with my dog
They melt and fade away

I'm the happiest man
With the happiest dog
At the happiest time of the day
The happiest man with the happiest dog
And everything's OK

Always pleased to see me
Waiting by my back door
This ever faithful friend I've found
Who could ask for more?

Sometimes he fetches sticks
But mostly a tennis ball
As long as he can race and chase
He doesn't care much at all

His ears are always bouncing
That tail goes to and fro
A bundle of joy – and boy oh boy
He's the happiest thing I know

Heaven is an open field
And if he had his way
He'd jump and run, having fun
All day, every day

He likes to hide in the long grass
But never strays too far
My faithful friend comes back again –
Oh what friends we are!

I'm the happiest man
With the happiest dog
At the happiest time of the day
The happiest man with the happiest dog
And everything's . . . OK

What is a Mermaid Made of?

Glittering shells, rainbow scales
The shimmer and glimmer of angelfish tails
The glow of a jellyfish, grace of a whale

The wishes of fishes, a breath of sea breeze
Seven blue shades from seven blue seas
A mermaid is made from a mixture of these

The Magician with Ambition

The magician with ambition
Was a mystical physician
Who sought the composition
Of a spell of great precision
For all things scientific
His knowledge was prolific
Voltage and transmission, gaseous ignition
Simple recognition of nuclear collision
And specific hieroglyphics
Was wicked and terrific

The wizard of decision
Was a great mathematician
A master statistician
Of addition and division
For all things mathematical
His brain was acrobatical
Fractions and subtractions, factors and reactions
Equation complications, long multiplications
Computations problematical
His mind was telepathical

The solution's constitution
Was brought unto fruition
Magic spells and sorcery
Defying definition
An amazing combination
Of enchanting calculations
A wonderful creation
Beyond imagination
A crazy composition of wish and superstition
Fulfilling the ambition of this magician's vision
The lotions and the potions
Made him such a rich 'un
Thanks to their transmission
On global television

Scarborough Summer Snapshots

Seagull vultures cry
a massed chorus of shrieking
echoing echoing echoing
like a needle stuck in a groove.

Clouds scurry by
on the vast blue underbelly of the sky
surfers on their own white waves.

Whispering grass, crackling paper
and the hollow empty laughter of Coca-Cola cans,
the only conversations on the wind-blown sea wall.

Incoming tide
blue with crescents white
spreading a cloak of beautiful deceit:
water in the open mouth
of sharp fanged teeth.

Racing on the crest of a breeze
clouds sprint like lemmings to the edge of the cliff
then fade and d
                i
                e.

Bodiless shirts billow
frantic and excited.
Limbless trousers run the races
of ten thousand marathons
yet never tire
fuelled by an invisible relentless force.

        Distant echoes
        laughter, shouting, ice-cream bells
        and seagull cries
        fade in then out of earshot
        like flies alighting on a page
        or the bright warm focus of the sun
        changing into shade.

The bright blue curtain of the sky
slowly closes from my view
as folding clouds billow
and slowly join together.

        Rippling teeth of waves
        comb the tussled beach.

Picnic leftovers
picked and looked over
pecked and lent over
by small brown sparrows.

Summer bright
Summer hot
Summer sunny
Summer not.

Sea Shoals See Shows on the Sea Bed

The salmon with a hat on
Was conducting with a baton
And it tried to tune a tuna fish
By playing on its scales
But the scales had all been flattened
When the tuna fish was sat on
On purpose by a porpoise
And a school of killer whales

So the salmon with a hat on
Fiddled with a baton
The angelfish got ready
To play the tambourine
Things began to happen
When the salmon with a baton
Was tapping out a pattern
For the band of the marines

There was a minnow on piano
A prawn with a horn
An otter on guitar
Looking all forlorn
A whale voice choir
A carp with a harp
A belly dancing jellyfish
Jiving with a shark

The octaves on the octopus
Played the middle eight
But they couldn't keep in time
With the skiffle-playing skate
The plaice on the bass
Began to rock and roll
With a bloater in a boater
And a Dover sole

A clam on castanets
An eel on glockenspiel
An oyster in a cloister
Singing with a seal
The haddock had a headache
From the deafening din
And the sword-dancing sword fish
Sliced off a fin

A limpet on a trumpet, a flatfish on a flute
The kipper fell asleep with King Canute
Barracuda on a tuba sat upon a rock
The electric eel gave everyone a shock

The shrimp and the sturgeon
The stingray and the squid
Sang a four-part harmony
On the sea bed
The crab and the lobster
Gave their claws a flick
Kept everyone in time
With a click click click

Kept everyone in time with a click click click . . .
Kept everyone in time with a click click click . . .

Yes the salmon with a hat on
Was tapping out a pattern
And things began to happen
For the band of the marines
It was an ocean of commotion of Atlantic
    proportion
The greatest show by schools of shoals
That ever had been seen

Bath Waters Run Deep

Dad did not smile nor did he laugh
Seeing the shark fin in the bath
Instead, began to fuss and fuss
When tickled by the octopus
His eyes could not believe it real
The shock of the electric eel
And then up popped the toilet lid
Shooting out a giant squid
His arms and legs began to flail
Until he saw the killer whale
He sat stock-still, too scared to move
The swordfish had a point to prove
It did so with a sharpened swish
And then dad saw the jellyfish
That shivered, shook and grew and grew
So dad began to shiver too
That was the least of current troubles
When bursting upwards through the bubbles
A mile of oily coils and – yes,
It was the monster from Loch Ness!
Dad wished he'd just washed in the sink
Bath water's deeper than you think
He also wished – and this is rude
He was not bathing in the nude
And since he was, his final wish

Was not to see piranha fish
Alas, these wishes don't come true
Piranha fish swam into view
A thousand spiky snapping teeth
That started biting underneath
A starfish then joined in the fun
At this point Dad began to run
So out he leaped with piercing howl
But could not find a single towel
A blur of pink and he was gone
Crabs and lobsters hanging on
So when you have a bath take care
Of monsters lurking everywhere
The moral of this tale will be
It's safer bathing in the sea!

Books at Bedtime

For Julia Donaldson

There have always been books,
Books at bedtime

Even as babies,
Colic afflicted, restless, coughing and crying

There have always been those books
Especially for that bedtime reading time

The Bible, *The Beano*, *Encyclopaedia Britannica*,
Treasure Island, *The Dandy*, Dickens and Dahl

Classics from every shelf
Stories from a different childhood

Tomes thick, volumes slim
The big, the small, the in-between

Illustrated picture books, sumptuous colours
Black and white lines, comic creations

All books at bedtime
Lulling the insomniac infant

Not just the reading of these million words
The telling of these thousand stories

Or the rhymes of a myriad lines
The rhythm of this children's garden of verse

As thick and thin lie side by side
Arranged on a hall floor

Literally a literary cobbled street
For a pram to undulate upon

The rock and roll of the wheels upon the words
The to and fro of the springs upon the stories

The osmosis of gentle lullabies
As words sing through the pages

In this secret midnight garden
Where a parent strolls perambulating

Perambulating on these special bedtime books
On the long, long, long road to slumberland

The wheels on the books go round and round
Round and round, round and round
All night long

HI-KU

Hello, how are you?
Greetings, ey up, now then you!
Hiya, how-do, hi!

BYE-KU

See you, ta-ra, ciao
Nice meeting you, tatty bye
Au revoir, next time

I Believe in Poetry

I believe in poetry
I believe in the word
Words never read are sleeping or dead
Words have a need to be heard
Because I believe in poetry

The poetry out of the ordinary
The poetry out of the everyday
The poetry out of the mundane
The poetry of cliché
Because I believe in poetry

The power of the line
Or the power of the rhyme
Those words that mark that moment in time
Those words sublime
They are yours and mine
Because I believe in poetry

The fun of a pun
But words are a gun
My tongue is the trigger – if I should pull it
Words of hate and words of hurt
Words are a speeding, unfeeling bullet

But words can bring us together
Or words can tear us apart
Words of feeling, words of healing
Words to melt the coldest heart
Words to melt the oldest heart
Words are always the place to start
Because I believe in poetry

Words that beseech
Words that can preach
Words that can teach
Or extend the hand of friendship
When they reach
Out . . . and about —
Words that shout
Words that whisper
Words that seduce
Words that kiss you
Because I believe in poetry

Words that fall away like dust
Or words that stand the test of time
That make you want that next line

Remembered and quoted
Published and noted
Words that shine a light
Words that ignite

Words that inspire
Words that touch our very souls
Words that light the fire
Words that take us even higher

Because we are creators
Gods and magicians
Spelling with letters
For words or for better
Better for words

Twenty-six alphabetical letters
Put them together for ever and ever
Mathematical combinations
Infinite configurations
Twenty-six letters defining our history
Twenty-six letters of magic and mystery
Twenty-six letters of possible tongue twistery

I believe in rhythms and rhyme
Alliteration and assonance
Syntax and simile
Metaphor, the metaphysical . . .
But most of all
I believe in words that sound dead good
When they are read out loud
Because I believe in poetry

I believe what a friend of mine said
If it doesn't sound good when it's read
Then it's not a very good poem

These words must have a voice
More than just their phonic noise
Once they have been spoken
Out in the open
The page is unlocked, the boundaries broken
Because I believe that poems
Can break down walls
I believe in poetry

I believe in the word
Words never read are sleeping or dead
Words have a need to be heard
Because I believe in poetry

Poet's Haiku

He just held the pen
The words appeared by magic
True and fully formed

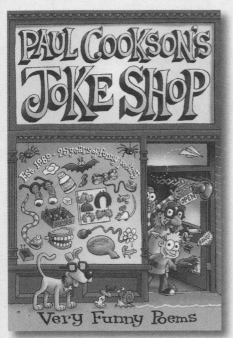

PAUL COOKSON'S JOKE SHOP

Est. 1989 - 25 years of funny poems

OPEN

BANG!

Very Funny Poems

100 Brilliant POEMS for Children

CHOSEN BY Paul Cookson

MACMILLAN POETRY

THE WORKS

EVERY KIND OF POEM YOU WILL EVER NEED AT SCHOOL

Chosen by PAUL COOKSON

OVER 200,000 COPIES SOLD

MACMILLAN POETRY

THE WORKS 3

A POET FOR EVERY WEEK OF THE YEAR

Chosen by PAUL COOKSON